It was one of those moments you never forget.

I'd been speaking at a weekend conference full of people dedicated to reading, studying, applying, and teaching the Bible. At the end of the conference, as we were all leaving, a man, probably in his 60s, his coat already buttoned, came up to me, looked me in the eye, and said,

"You just validated my whole life."

I was speechless. I was completely taken aback, confused, bewildered actually. I must have looked it because he then went on, "You see I worked in insurance." And before I could say anything at all, the man in the coat left.

But I understood. It wasn't because I'd offered the conference a robust biblical theology of insurance. In fact, I don't think I mentioned the word 'insurance' at all. I'd been speaking on Colossians 1 and 3, Genesis 1, Ruth 2 and Acts 27. And the man in the coat had probably read and perhaps studied all those passages before. But over that weekend the Spirit of God illuminating those passages had assured him that the God he had given his life to had been interested in his life's work all along. All those years in insurance had counted for something in his heavenly Father's eyes. He hadn't wasted his life.

Id,

....- pursue his priorities.

There was Maddie, 73-ish, socially distanced in the supermarket queue, thinking what a bore, what a faff. And then it hit her, right there in the car park. 'God could work here. Why not? And I could join in.' So, she prayed before every trip to the supermarket. And a ministry began.

There was Sunita, 26, who thought that her medical research was irrelevant to Christ. Then a friend visiting her lab taught her why her research was so in line with God's purposes. And right there in her lab, she wept with relief and joy.

There was Josh, 23, who thought that God couldn't care two pins about his job in the factory. And then... I could go on.

All those people were affected by a false belief about God. All of them were affected by the great divide.

* The 98%/95% calculation is based on approx. 2% of church-attendees in the UK working in church-paid work. Of 168 hours in the week, approx. 120 are waking hours, with average church activities per week estimated at 3–10 hours.

Are you affected by the great divide?

The great divide is the all-too-common belief that some parts of our life are sacred and really important to God – prayer, Sunday services, church-based activities – but that others are secular and irrelevant to God – work, school, university, sport, the arts, music, rest, sleep, hobbies. It's a lie that distorts God's character and severely limits our everyday enjoyment of him. Tragically, it also severely limits our understanding of our everyday role in God's purposes.

It is because of this sacred–secular divide that study after study reveals that the vast majority of Christians do not feel equipped for mission in their daily contexts, nor helped to know Christ's presence with them where they spend most of their time.

Yes, in the last thirty years, the UK church has taken an amazing range of fruitful initiatives in evangelism, in social action, in youth work, in resource development, in a host of areas. However, the number of people regularly attending our churches has plummeted. Monthly UK church attendance has declined markedly – from 8.5% of the population in 1990, 7.1% in 2000, 6.6% in 2010 to 5.4% (pre-Covid) in 2020. But that conceals regional variations. Pre-Covid, it was 19.2% in Northern Ireland, 6.6% in Scotland, 4.9% in England and 4.3% in Wales. Globally, almost every Western nation has seen significant decline over the last twenty years.

But imagine what the situation might be if all God's people – kids, teens, students, workers, parents, carers, volunteers, unemployed, retired – imagine if all of us had been envisioned for our mission and ministry where we naturally engage with people who don't know Jesus day by day – in person or on Zoom? What if we all had a vision, and the training and the support for our everyday ministry beyond the church building?

But, on the whole, we don't. As one teacher put it:

'I spend an hour a week teaching Sunday school and they haul me up to the front of the church to pray for me. The rest of the week I'm a full-time teacher and the church has never prayed for me.'

This sidelining of everyday ministry is definitely not intentional.

You'd be hard-pressed to find a Christian leader anywhere in the UK who wouldn't agree that all of life is important to God. But there's a big difference between knowing something in your head and living it out in your everyday life. Most of us know that exercise and a good diet are really good for our physical and mental health but that doesn't mean we're all taking regular exercise and shovelling in the fruit and veg.

Similarly, the conviction that everything matters to God is not necessarily reflected in what we teach and sing and pray when we gather in our church communities.

That is the power of this sacred-secular divide – we know it's not true, but it carries on doing its damaging work anyway.

The sacred–secular divide (SSD) is the malignant foe of fruitful mission and joyful Christian living across the globe. Since this essay was first published in 2010, more and more people have begun to address this vital issue, but SSD is a potent enemy whose poisonous influence has penetrated almost every aspect of church life. And that makes it both more important and more urgent that we totally eradicate it, and that we do not allow it to shape our post-Covid understanding of mission and discipleship.

There is, after all, a better way, a richer truth, and a life more abundant for every follower of Jesus to enjoy. And share.

> That is the power of this sacred-secular divide. We know it's not true, but it carries on doing its damaging work anyway.

*Figures and projections from
Does the Future have a Church? by Peter

Pause for
a moment.

> Why do so many
> of us believe that
> church-paid ministry
> is a higher calling
> than any other?

> Why do we pray for
> teens on short-term
> mission trips, but
> not, or rarely, for
> their daily mission in
> their own school?

> Why do so few of us
> feel equipped for
> ministry and mission
> in our daily work?

> Why are so few
> worship songs about
> God in our daily lives?

These are all
symptoms of
the sacred-
secular divide.

READING THE SIGNS

Now, popular analysis of the reasons for the church's decline in the West has tended to focus on external factors – ideological, economic, and cultural.

Ideologically, shifts in ways of viewing the world have tended to relegate faith to the private sphere. Religious faith is seen as a matter for personal, inward reflection. It's one option among many around which to shape private life choices but certainly not the basis for significant public policy decisions, nor for shaping the values of our workplaces or institutions.

Other commentators point to the power of consumerism, which vaunts material things not only as pleasurable – which they often are – but also as sources of identity, self-esteem, and belonging. Nike ergo sum. I wear Nike, therefore I am. I wear Nike, therefore I can be part of the group.

Others blame the media, the web, and the myriad forms of entertainment, communication, and distraction – the new opiates of the masses – which anaesthetise us from our alienation and pain and prevent us dealing with that most awkward thing, ourselves.

The problem with these diagnoses is that they tend to suggest that the gospel of the crucified and resurrected Jesus is impotent to resist the onslaught of these external forces, never mind offer a credible, transformative alternative. In other words, we blame the world for the demise of Christian values in the world, and perhaps don't ask ourselves to what extent we might be responsible. LICC's founder John Stott said, 'You can't blame the meat for going rotten. That's what meat does. You blame the salt for not being there to preserve it.'

So, the question is this: Is our mission being constrained not so much by the potency of false ideas outside the church, but by the potency of false ideas inside the church?

Yes, we should rejoice in all that local churches are doing in their communities. Who's running parent and toddler groups? Who's voluntarily helping people with drugs, drink, and debt? Who's got afternoon clubs for school kids with working parents and carers, and clubs on Saturdays for divorced dads and their kids? Who's staffing foodbanks and voluntarily visiting old people in their homes…? The answer, in many communities, is Christians in the local church. It's an extraordinary contribution to social capital through formal programmes and millions of acts of spontaneous kindness.

On the other hand, if we ask ourselves, 'Am I or are the people in my church having an impact for Christ in the places where we naturally spend time during the week?' then many would answer, 'A bit, I think.'

Some of that is simply lack of awareness of how God has almost certainly been working through us. Nevertheless, given the state of our country and institutions, Christian influence on the character of our national and community life is clearly far, far less than what the gospel demands. After all, wherever we are – classroom, school gate, kitchen, gym, field, factory, office – we all have an opportunity to live out God's values of kindness, truthfulness, and justice. We all have the opportunity to seek to be a blessing where we are, to help create a more enriching culture, and to bring God's wisdom to the challenges we face, and, in God's time, to share the hope that we have in Christ. But SSD has largely obliterated that vision. Life shouldn't be divided into self-contained segments, some of which are important to God and others of which are not. Life's a peach, not an orange. It's all significant to God. And in him it all hangs together.

The divide teaches
us that there is a
*hierarchy of
holiness in
work.*

The sacred-secular divide leads us to believe that really holy people become overseas missionaries, moderately holy people become local church pastors, and people who are not much use to God get a job. Bah humbug. Of course, this is not something that many missionaries or pastors themselves consciously believe or would, indeed, ever say. But the reality is that the majority of Christians do have a sense that they are second-class citizens of the kingdom of heaven, and that all the hours they spend in non-church activities each week (about 110, excluding sleep) are not of any substantial interest to the God who created the world he calls us to steward.

The sacred-secular divide tells us that 98% of us are not missionaries, ministers, or full-time Christian workers. It tells us that pretty much any job – from ad exec to bricklayer, cleaner to delivery driver, welder to zookeeper – doesn't really matter to God, except as a context to share the gospel.

The divide tells us that all Christians may be born equal but full-time Christian workers are more equal than others.

It's a lie.

Did Jesus call any of us to be a part-time Christian worker? Or to take up our cross daily, but only when we get home from work or school?

It's a lie.

Beyond that, the sacred-secular divide teaches us that there is a hierarchy of holiness even among the 98% of non-church-paid Christians. SSD teaches us that the caring professions – nursing, social work, teaching – are inherently more valuable to God than industry or commerce. Indeed, it's because of SSD that the church has historically often treated business with some distaste, failing to recognise that the poor need jobs, not just aid, and that there is no poverty alleviation without wealth generation. As one businessman put it: 'The church appreciates my tithe but not the enterprise that gives rise to it.' Yes, the Covid pandemic woke us all up, Christians and not, to the value of a whole host of jobs – not just medics but cleaners, truck drivers, supermarket workers, transport workers, postal workers, sanitation workers, teachers, hairdressers... but this new appreciation has not been born of an understanding of God's view of work, but rather by the grim reality of our circumstances.

More generally, SSD foments dissatisfaction with our contexts and ourselves: 'Oh, if only I were elsewhere, then God could use me!', 'If only I were holier, then God would call me to pastoral ministry or overseas mission.' The result is that we don't embrace our contexts, or look to see where God is already at work and how we might join in. The grass is not greener somewhere else, the grass is greener where it is watered – with biblical vision, faith-filled expectation, and God's blessing. Even

Christians in healthcare can be beset by SSD – leading many to suppose that the highest calling, after church work, is to overseas medical mission. One psychologist I've encountered has even thought about leaving the profession because, except in very rare instances, they can't share the gospel with their patients in their day job.

Now if we don't believe that our daily work is significant to God, we will be all the more driven to maximise the amount of time we give to serving in our local church. Of course, that's good to do but not if it leads to burn-out, and not if it's because we believe that we haven't done anything significant for God anywhere else.

The abundant life in Jesus embraces every aspect of our life.

And whatever we do we are all called to the challenge and the joy of working with God to make the world a better place, to produce goods and services that benefit people to the glory of God, to alleviate poverty by creating jobs as well as offering aid, to work to release potential through endeavour – sand into silicon chips, children into confident adults, disparate individuals into productive teams, and, by God's grace, sceptics into followers of Jesus. What a relief it is when we know that we're in the right place already and that God has a purpose for us – right where we are.

The divide affects everyone – kids, teens, students, workers, mums, dads, retirees – everyone.

It is because of the sacred-secular divide that a teenager can go to a superb youth conference with thousands of 12 to 18-year-olds, be encouraged by stunning Bible teaching, engaged in God-honouring worship, offered life-changing prayer, given a vision for a life of active service in God's purposes for the world, but never hear the word 'school' in relation to those purposes, never have the call to mission and discipleship connected to the place where they spend a huge proportion of their waking time.

In fact, SSD not only affects what we teach in church, it affects our attitude to education in general. It is because of SSD that there's hardly a child or adult or youth worker who could give you a biblical perspective on maths, even though every child in the land spends several hours a week on maths for at least 11 years. It is because of SSD that Christian commentators have thought long and hard about 'supernatural' stories like *Harry Potter, Twilight, His Dark Materials* – primarily leisure-time reading – but have almost entirely ignored the literature our teenagers study at GCSE which may actually be deeply opposed to gospel values. On the whole, we don't help our children think biblically about what they study, nor help them embrace their education, as Daniel did, as a vital preparation for their service in God's world.

SSD affects student life too. So it is that a grateful graduate of a fine university could say of their otherwise very supportive, highly purposeful Christian Union: 'The CU completely ignored why we were at university.' That is, the CU failed to help Christian students engage biblically with their studies. And this narrowness in turn affects the potency of students' evangelistic efforts. Emerging generations are looking for a way of living that works. And people who aren't Christians need to see and hear a whole-life gospel that makes a difference to how Christian students study, house-share, date, eat, drink, and are merry.

Similarly, it's because of SSD that the vast majority of mums and dads do not feel that theirs is a high calling on the frontline of disciplemaking. In reality, they not only have the opportunity to nurture their own children to become disciples who can have a long-term impact on the nation, they also have the potential for significant outreach to other parents met at ante-natal classes, kids' birthday parties, and so on. Sadly, whilst many churches support parent and toddler groups, they don't tend to honour and celebrate them as enthusiastically as other forms of disciplemaking and mission.

It's because of SSD that many retired Christians are particularly grateful that they can give much more of their time to church-related activities because those really do matter to God. Indeed, even though they may offer time and skills to all kinds of activities in their communities, they are much less likely, because of SSD, to see those activities, or even their engagement with their grandkids, as kingdom work. And that means they are less likely to pray about it or ask others to.

It **blinds** us to
seeing what is
plainly visible
in the Bible.

Our work,
our life,
matters.

The sacred-secular divide has shaped the way we read the Bible, the way we have been taught to study the Bible, and the way our pastors have been trained to teach the Bible.

So, for example, study after study, informal survey after informal survey have revealed that preaching and teaching in local churches tends to be least helpful for the contexts where people spend most time – work, for example. Why, in the case of work, might that be?

After all, there is a huge amount of material in the Bible from Genesis to Revelation that's about work or that can be applied to work. It's as creator/worker that God is first introduced to us – Genesis 1:1. It's work that is the primary task that Adam is given to do – to release the potential of God's creation even as he cares for it – Genesis 2:15. Work is an intrinsic part of the way the biblical story unfolds. It is in the story of Cain and Abel. It's in the first big construction project – the ark – and in the second – the tower of Babel. Similarly, we are invited to think about Abraham's dealings as a wealthy herdsman, to reflect on Jacob's transactions with Laban, Joseph's managerial role under Potiphar and Pharaoh, Moses' leadership, Jethro's consultancy, Deborah's judgeship, Ruth and Boaz's labour in the fields... and so on all the way through the Bible where we discover that there will be work, though no toil, in the new creation (Micah 4:3; Isaiah 65:21–23).

How is it that a biblical view of work and working has not been taught?

And how is it that the vast majority of Christians haven't seen it for themselves?

After all, work is not some peripheral issue, or some topic that has only popped onto our screens in the last five years. Work – paid and unpaid purposeful activity that contributes to the common good – is something that everyone does. Indeed, the vast majority of people spend a huge chunk of their lives engaged in work as employees. Furthermore, work is critical to the flourishing of every community and every nation. You would therefore expect us to be particularly alert to it when we read our Bibles. But overall the opposite is true.

That is the power of SSD. It blinds us to seeing what is plainly visible in the Bible.

The problem, however, is not only that SSD has blinded us to seeing work as biblically significant, it has blinded us to seeing all of everyday life as biblically significant.

In the beginning God created the heavens and the earth.

It's as a creator – a worker – that God is first introduced to us.

The failure, for example, to teach work well is part of a wider failure to offer a whole-life gospel to non-believers. No wonder so many people, especially in the West, fail to be truly gripped by the gospel. The gospel we've been presenting rarely includes any compelling vision for the transformation of ordinary daily life, wherever people spend time, whatever they do. And it ignores the means by which such transformation is possible.

This is particularly important for young people between 14 and 35. As research has shown, they are yearning for an authentic, whole-life vision for their lives. They don't want to be one person on Monday and another on Sunday. They don't just want a job. They want purposeful work that makes a positive difference to people's lives and the planet we inhabit. They don't just want to live for the weekend. They want to live for today. And make something beautiful of it.

How can anyone remain interested in a religion which seems to have no concern with nine-tenths of his life?

The great writer and thinker
Dorothy L. Sayers put it
that way, back in 1942.

They want their whole lives to count.

And in Christ, of course, they *do*.

The gospel is not just a dazzling invitation to forgiveness of sin and eternal life in the glorious presence of the triune God. It is a divine summons to join a movement to change the world in and through all they are in Christ and all they do in Christ, Monday to Sunday, in the places the Lord already has them. SSD has, however, left us with a shrunken vision and that is reflected in how we do church together.

A few years ago I was asked by Graham Kendrick, the great Christian singer-songwriter and worship leader, to analyse the themes and theology of contemporary hymns and songs, with particular reference to whole-life discipleship. His concern was this: 'Are we perpetuating an abstract spirituality?' Broadly speaking, the answer to his question was, 'Yes'. You certainly won't find many songs that express the kind of gritty engagement with daily life that you find in David's psalms, with his frequent references to his work and the tools of his trade, and his constant alertness to God's involvement and intervention in his daily life as shepherd, soldier, husband, adulterer, fugitive, father, general, king...

Similarly, SSD affects our prayer life, individual and corporate. How rare it is for congregational prayer to include issues facing people in their Monday to Saturday contexts beyond the domestic. (Or their Sunday contexts, if that's a working day.) And while a home group may well pray by name for the church's overseas missionaries, it might never even know the names of the boss or colleague or grandchild of anyone in the group, never mind pray for them.

The sacred-secular divide limits our sense of where God might work, and how he might work. Yes, God may heal someone physically in a sanctuary or a home group, but does it occur to us that he might heal on the factory floor or in the offices of an advertising agency? Well, he certainly healed my former boss's PA in my Madison Avenue office. Furthermore, the idea that Jesus might actually be discipling us in our primary arena of occupation rarely hits our radar. But where are the challenges to Christlike character more acute – in a factory or a home Bible study? In which context is it more difficult to display the fruit of the Spirit or think in ways that do not conform to the surrounding culture?

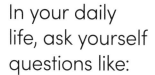

In your daily life, ask yourself questions like:

How have I seen God's hand at work here?

What is God teaching me?

What do I sense he might be doing here?

How does my faith change how I view this place?

And let's ask *each other*, 'Where do you spend your time in the week?' and then support each other for the contexts we find ourselves in. Right now, on the whole, we aren't.

Indeed, you can see the impact of a focus on leisure-time in the way that SSD affects the practice of our devotional life. Think, for a moment, about how much devotional material revolves around taking time away from the frontline of family, work, and school – quiet times, fasting, silence, retreats. All these are healthy spiritual disciplines of separation. But there's been much less emphasis on material that helps us connect to God, hear his voice, and practise his presence in the midst of life, out on the frontline: the spiritual disciplines of engagement. Prayer is 5G – anywhere, anytime.

The impact of SSD goes deeper still.

It affects our understanding of our very humanity.

SSD makes people believe that art, music, and the multifarious ways in which human beings express their God-given human creativity have no place in the kingdom of God – unless they have overtly Christian themes.

Similarly, SSD leads to a negative view of the body, and of physical pleasures. By contrast, the Bible affirms the material world as created by God, reminds us that Jesus had a body and does still, promises that eternal life includes a new resurrection body and involves a new earth, as well as new heavens. The Bible also celebrates the emotional and psychological pleasures of good wine, bread, and oil, not just their physiological benefits. Wine is given to 'gladden the heart', Psalm 104 tells us, not just to reduce the likelihood of a heart attack. And it is surely not merely for symbolic reasons that Jesus' first sign in John's Gospel was to provide a great deal of rather excellent wine to keep a wedding party humming.

SSD, however, ignores the way the Bible affirms enjoyment of the beauty of God's creation and of people's creativity and prowess. They're refreshing, restorative, providential gifts from our heavenly Father. So we're free to relish the rich, relaxed 'chook-chook-chook' of a blackbird, the breathtaking originality of Hendrix's guitar solo in *All Along the Watchtower*, a really good joke, or the velvety smooth sweetness of a Lindor chocolate.

In our Creator's good world, none of this is a waste of time.

Indeed, holiness, as the book of Leviticus makes abundantly clear, is far from being some ethereal, otherworldly spirituality. Holiness manifests itself in how we live out our lives in the physical world. It's about disease control (Leviticus 12–16); godly relationships (Leviticus 18); honest scales and weights (Leviticus 19:36); telling the truth, avoiding slander (Leviticus 19:11, 16); ensuring the poor have food (Leviticus 19:9) – doing all to the glory of God.

This is not about giving God's people some teaching on a few key topics, but about giving God's people new eyes to see the scope of their calling as followers of Jesus.

Living in the grip of the
great divide is like squinting
at the Champs-Élysées
through a millimetre crack.
What you can see looks great.

But imagine what it
feels like when the
door is flung open.

The sacred-secular divide ~~limits~~ our outreach.

It limits the mission's location

to near the church building or far, far away.

It limits the mission's messengers

telling us it's only for church staff and missionaries.

It limits the mission's time

tending to confine it to our evenings and weekends.

It limits the mission's message

to one that's not about all our life and all our being.

That is why SSD is the greatest challenge facing the church. Far from 'the whole church taking the whole gospel to the whole world', we have a small percentage of the church taking a partial gospel to far, far fewer people than are actually known by the Christians in our congregations. Indeed, in 2010, at the fourth Lausanne Congress on World Evangelization, I suggested that the primary mission strategy of the church seemed to be: 'To recruit the people of God to give up some of their leisure time to support the mission initiatives of church-paid workers.'

There were representatives from over 190 countries there. Virtually everyone agreed that this was the strategy they had in their country. It's certainly the primary one we've had in Britain for the last fifty years. And what it has meant is that the 98% of us who aren't in church paid work have been neither envisioned nor equipped for mission in 95% of our waking lives.

But just imagine if we were.

The divide is like putting a red sock in a white wash. Everything comes out pink. And so everything needs rewashing.

EMBRACING THE WHOLE-LIFE GOSPEL

'For by him all things were created: things in heaven and on earth, visible and invisible, whether thrones or powers or rulers or authorities; all things were created by him and for him.'

Colossians 1:16

At its root, the divide stems from a distorted and incomplete view of God.

It limits the apparent scope of God's concern to a very narrow band of activities, and thereby blinkers our vision of how wide and long and high and deep is his love. And how glorious he is. SSD makes us think that God is like a parent who is only interested in one aspect of our lives, say, our academic performance. Yes, they help us with our homework, discuss ideas with us, fund relevant trips, and encourage us to work hard, sleep well, and eat lots of fish. And we really appreciate them for that. But they aren't interested in our love of tennis, or Taylor Swift, or *Schitt's Creek*, or green fashion, or giraffes, or our entrepreneurial ability to make money selling snacks in school breaks. Wouldn't it be so much better to have a parent who is interested in all of our life? A parent who can see how all these areas might be an opportunity to engage with us and help us grow, even if they'd rather be listening to medieval lute music than Taylor Swift in the car?

In fact, our Father in heaven is interested in all of our life. We see it in the beauty of the surroundings he created for Adam and Eve in Eden. We see it in his intense interest in what Adam would name the animals and the birds. We see it in

his tenderness as he makes clothes for his naked, rebellious children; we see it throughout the Bible. And we see his interest in all things supremely in the work of his Son on the cross.

In Colossians 1:15, Paul affirms that Jesus 'is the image of the invisible God, the firstborn over all creation'. He then clarifies why: 'For by him all things were created: things in heaven and on earth...all things were created by him and for him' (v 16). Visible things – toucans, elephants, bananas – and things invisible – wind, thought, power. Now here are two reasons for Jesus' abiding interest in the material world:

One: He created it.
Two: He created it for himself.

If 'all things' were created by and for Christ, why wouldn't he be interested in the impact that our activities in the kitchen, at school, in factories, fields, and offices have on his creation?

However, the climax of Paul's argument is not a robust theology of divine creation, but a startling affirmation of the comprehensive scope of Jesus' work on the cross. God is working through Jesus: 'to reconcile to himself all things, whether things on earth or things in heaven, by making peace through his blood, shed on the cross' (v 20). Jesus' sacrifice is not only intended to offer all human beings the opportunity for reconciliation with him, but to reconcile all things, all matter, the entire cosmos to himself. Jesus' work on the cross serves to bring all things back into proper relationship with him

Similarly, in Revelation 21:5, he who is seated on the throne says, 'I am making everything new!' God is not saying that he is going to obliterate all that he has created and start again. Rather he is promising to transform all things. The earth will be renewed, not replaced. So, when Peter writes that 'the present heavens and earth are reserved for fire' (2 Peter 3:7), he means that, they will be cleansed of evil, rather in the way that a farmer might burn off the stubble in a field to make way for a new crop. Indeed, the flood (2 Peter 3:6) does not obliterate planet earth, but it does create the possibility of a new beginning. So, in the Gospel of John, we see that the resurrected Jesus has a 'new' body with new potential (John 20–21) but it is still recognisably the body he had in his earthly life. And God's new creation promises to supersede in its beauty and glory even the heart-stopping beauty of a scarlet macaw or the Kyoto cherry blossom or a Bora Bora lagoon.

SSD then denies God's intentions for creation and the new creation, and, as we shall now see, severely limits our understanding of our role in the mission of God.

Yes, Jesus came to die to satisfy the wrath of a holy, loving Father, to take away the sin of the world. He came so that many would be rescued from futility and hell, so that many would come to know him and love him and spend time and eternity with him. But he also came that we might have abundant life, life to the full. And he calls his servants to cooperate with him in making his world as much like he intends it to be before he returns. The prayer, 'Your kingdom come, your will be done on earth as it is in heaven' is a prayer for today, even if it will only be fully realised in the future. 'Your kingdom come, your will be done in my office, my school, my football club, my local council, my home...'

This is the great project – the reconciliation and renewal of God's world.

And God calls all of us to be involved in it.

Indeed, when SSD is replaced by a whole-life ethos it enables us to begin to see the imaginative possibilities of ordinary life lived with gospel resources. So, the challenge to the twenty-first-century church is not one that can be addressed by a new set of programmes. Rather, it is one that must be addressed by the rediscovery of a whole-life Christianity that, in turn, will shape all our attitudes and activities.

Our picture of the church in the ghetto, in the corner, is replaced by the realisation that Monday to Saturday the people of God are not hemmed into a corner but out in the world, touching scores of lives in a whole variety of ways.

You certainly have lots of contacts if you're a member of a club or take your children to school, or go shopping or live in a retirement home, or if you go to school or university or work, even if it's mostly via Zoom. As the World Council of Churches put it in 1954: 'The real battles of faith today are being fought in factories, shops, offices and farms, in political parties and government agencies, in countless homes, in press, radio and television, in the relationship of nations. Very often it is said the church should "go into these spheres" but the fact is that the church is already in these spheres in the persons of its laity.'

In reality, the majority of Christians are already in potentially fruitful contexts for witness and mission. Their workplace, for example, not only offers the opportunity to develop relationships through which people may meet Jesus, but can also play a significant role in social transformation. After all, if we want better schools, shaped by Christian values, we will need teachers whose teaching is shaped by the Bible. If we want justice in our courts, we will have to look to lawyers and the police. If we want better mental health care, we will need doctors and administrators to shape and deliver it. If we want trust in business, we had better start where we work.

Indeed, a whole-life perspective enables us to see that every context we find ourselves in is not just a place to display Christian character – to model the virtues of Jesus – but also a place to minister grace and love to others, to mould the culture we're in, to be a mouthpiece for truth and justice, and to be a messenger of the gospel.

After all, a Christian secretary in an office may, over time, have many an opportunity to 'pastor' their colleagues; a manager may have many an opportunity to offer wisdom and comfort to people suffering through a crisis; and an 11-year-old starting secondary school has seven years to develop relationships that may last a lifetime and may lead some of their friends to everlasting life before the ink is dry on their last 'A' level exam.

We are not hemmed in – we are salt and light.

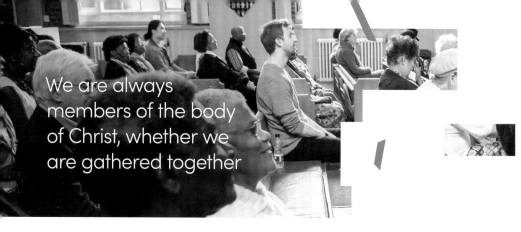

We are always
members of the body
of Christ, whether we
are gathered together

When is the body of Christ the body of Christ? In current practice, the answer often is when we are doing things together – either physically in the church building or organised from the church building. Despite recent growing affirmation of the ministry and priesthood of all believers, this is almost always understood as the ministry and priesthood of all believers acting within the local church community. However, a whole-life perspective changes how we see ourselves, and others, in the body of Christ.

Indeed, all the things we do together as the gathered community of God's people – our teaching, our worship in song, our sharing in the bread and wine, our praying together – should both lead us to engage more richly with the living God and also thereby help shape us for fruitful living in the world.

We are always members of the body of Christ, whether we are gathered in a Sunday service or scattered on our frontlines in the world. Even if we are the only Christian when we go to a coffee morning, or work, or the shops, we still go as the individual representative of Christ's body. So we should actively seek the prayers and support of our brothers and sisters for those contexts, and we should actively look for ways to encourage others in their roles, both in and beyond church activities, and learn how we can do things 'together', even when we are physically apart.

We might formally commission plumbers for their work, or people who are about to retire into a new phase of service for the king of kings, or school kids for their mission and ministry in their school. We might put local clubs and shops and businesses on our prayer lists, along with the homeless project and the Monday evening football sessions for teens. More simply, we might just get to know each other a bit better and celebrate our various enthusiasms.

or scattered
in the world.

One of the reasons many Christians have lost confidence in the gospel is because we may not have a testimony of how Jesus has indeed helped us in our ordinary everyday lives. And that tends to make us less enthusiastic to share the good news with others. After all, if my neighbour's number one issue is their fractious marriage and I don't have wisdom from the Bible or a testimony of how God has helped me or someone else in our marriage or relationships, then what kind of good news do I have to offer? Yes, I still have the truth to proclaim, but do I have a 'way' to point to and 'life' to testify to? Similarly, if my colleague's number one issue is their stressful job and I can't share a testimony of how God helps people in times of pressure, then what kind of gospel do I have to offer? Yes, I still have a wonderful truth to proclaim, but will I be confident to proclaim it when I don't believe that Jesus really can help my colleague with their life issues?

So a recovery of the whole-life gospel leads us to expect that Jesus wants to help us in every aspect of our life, and so to change us to become more like him. Jesus expects us to help one another discover and appropriate the lavish resources of word and Spirit and fellowship that will enable us to live out the gospel of abundant life: God helping us to turn difficult relationships into purposeful companionship; repetitive, even boring work into fruitful service for the king of the universe; pay rises into opportunities for generosity.

God transforms
the ordinary.

And that gives us much
more confidence to
talk about Jesus.

He's not just an idea, he's a living person who transforms people's lives today – see what the Lord has done. After all, as we have seen, many people today – Christian and not – are looking for an integrated way of life that empowers them to be consistent in values and action in every area of life – and therefore to be authentic. And that is precisely the kind of life Jesus lived and wants for us all.

LIVING WITHOUT THE DIVIDE

So, how shall we move forward?

Let us rediscover the riches of the whole-life gospel, and figure out together how to live it and disciple others in it too. Not that this will be easy. It's not easy for a ten-year-old to change the culture of her primary school. But she did. It's not easy for someone confined to her home to see how she can minister to those who don't know Jesus. But she did. It's not easy for a retired professional to obey God's command to pick up litter and trust him for the results. But he did. It's not easy for a retailer to forego the profit from a popular product by refusing to sell it on moral grounds. But he did. It's not easy for a mum to turn the hurly burly of the schoolgate into a context

for outreach and care. But she did. It's not easy for a boss to know when the moment is right to invite someone in his team to an evangelistic course but he prayed, and gave her the invitation. And within 18 months, she'd come to know Christ. Testimonies abound.

We should not underestimate the profound impact a whole-life gospel orientation will have on us as individuals, on our churches, and on our collective potential to make an impact on our society. This will undoubtedly take us beyond our comfort zones. Yet, as we seek to live all of life before the Lord, we will, by his grace and Spirit, become different people.

We need a radical return to whole-life disciplemaking.

As it relates to the local church, we need a radical return to whole-life disciplemaking as the central task of the body of Christ. At least, that's what we need if we want to win more than skirmishes and make sure that the next generation of Christians are better equipped to live and share the whole-life good news than we are now. As Bishop Graham Cray put it at an LICC event: 'Churches have to realise that the core of their calling is to be disciplemaking communities whatever else they do.'

And that has profound implications for the focus and orientation of ministerial training and theological education.

Indeed, it's because of the need to help churches become whole-life disciplemaking communities that LICC began a project back in 2004 designed to help local churches bring about the profound shift in culture and practice that is required to root out SSD and make whole-life disciplemaking central and sustainable in the life of the church. And we've seen that it is possible – in churches small and large, urban, suburban and rural, Anglican, Baptist, Pentecostal, Presbyterian, Methodist, new churches... it is possible. And it is happening.

Still, we are under no illusions. SSD has been in the church's bloodstream for nearly two millennia, and it will not give up its dominion without a fight. It will be hard to defeat precisely because it affects every aspect of church culture. It won't be uprooted by sermons alone – though it is unlikely to be uprooted without a renewed grasp of what the Bible has to say about God's comprehensive vision for human flourishing. Still, it won't be uprooted by sermons alone because the likelihood is that the prayer life, the worship life, the group life, the conversational life of the church will still be brimming with the culture of SSD, and will quench the sparks of whole-life discipleship that the sermons might have ignited. To change a culture you always need to change more than one thing.

Furthermore, SSD will also not be overcome merely by earnest effort, multiple initiatives, and biblically-based reasoning – though all are required.

The sacred-
secular divide
**is a way of
thinking and
living that we
need to repent of.**

**None of us
are immune.**

Yes, we may be entirely convinced
that all of life really matters to God
and yet most of our churches are
affected by SSD. And I certainly
keep discovering blind spots in
my own life. It is after all, one
thing to know something and it's
another to live it. Getting rid of
SSD is a process. But repentance
is the first and decisive step on the
path to healing and wholeness,
the path to renewed joy in God,
and to living with eyes of wonder
and gratitude in his world.

We need consciously and prayerfully to turn away from this flawed thinking that has so limited our understanding of the scope of Jesus' interest in his world, and that has so falsely represented the glorious riches of the good news. It has become part of our system and so perhaps we should bring this false system to the Lord, confess it, seek his forgiveness, and crave his blessing for a different future.

Lord have mercy, Christ have mercy.

Perhaps, too, some of us have colluded with the system – we've known that God was a God of all of life and have chosen not to pursue what would inevitably be a more difficult, more costly path. We've been content, or perhaps resigned, to being spectators in the stands, not participants in the adventure. Or perhaps we've had an intimation that there must be more to the Christian life than the Christian life we've been leading, and we've suppressed that thought.

Lord have mercy, Christ have mercy.

Perhaps we've sat in church services Sunday after Sunday listening to stories of pastors and overseas missionaries and social activists and known that there was more, that there were tales to be told of schoolchildren and builders, cleaners and accountants that would never be told. And worse, that there were people who, as one NHS worker put it to me, would 'die without knowing the ministry God had for them'. And we knew. But we weren't prepared to challenge the status quo for fear of offending the leadership or bringing disunity.

Lord have mercy, Christ have mercy.

Perhaps we've been in church leadership and we know that God has called us to make disciples for all of life and we have not had the stomach to take on what we assume will be stiff congregational resistance to such a path. Perhaps we've preferred to recruit volunteers for leisure-time initiatives rather than propel disciples into whole-life mission. Perhaps we haven't really had the confidence that God can work through our people to further his kingdom where they are – in that factory job they hate, with the grandchild they have lunch with every week, in that secondary school where they're the only Christian in their form. Perhaps we haven't really been interested to go and see if he is already working.

Imagine shalom.

Imagine what might happen if all God's people were envisioned and equipped and supported in their everyday mission. What a difference that might make to the people they know, to the organisations they serve, to the towns and cities and nations they are part of and, indeed, to themselves. We have all been created to be part of the adventure of the mission of God, to abide in him and let him transform every aspect of our lives. Jesus is Lord of all.

The potential impact of breaking down SSD is to release hundreds of thousands – millions – of ordinary Christians into the epic purposes of God. The potential is to see whole communities of God's people envisioned and equipped and supported for whole-life mission and discipleship in the places where they spend most of their time, among the people they already know. Of course, living out the whole-life gospel may sound all rather daunting but it begins with little things – praying about an area of your life you normally ignore, inviting a church leader to visit you at work, asking someone to tell you their life story, discovering a child's enthusiasms or a teenager's favourite film or song, looking back on the day through God's eyes... little things that help you pay attention to people and places and what God might be saying through it all.

The gospel is holistic. It affects all of life and it affects every aspect of who we are. The light is intended to shine through every pane of glass in the stained-glass window. It affects our minds, our hearts, and our bodies because God calls on us to love him thus, with our minds and our hearts and our bodies. And so our testimony and our service to the watching, listening world will be holistic – 'taste and see that the Lord is good', in all his ways.

Indeed, the Hebrew concept of shalom relates to all of life. Its essential meaning is not peace. Its essential meaning is wholeness – the fruitfulness that comes to all of life when we're in healthy relationship with God, our neighbours, all of nature, and our inner selves. At LICC, we yearn that God's people might know true shalom of heart, mind, and body, day by day and hour by hour. And we hope that you will join us in praying, in wrestling with Scripture, in creative experiments, and in generous sharing of what you're discovering so that together we might learn how to live, share, and proclaim this life of shalom in Christ wherever the Lord has placed us.

In all your ways, may you walk in step with the Prince of Shalom, and be empowered by his Spirit, so that our Father's name might be hallowed and his will be done as in heaven so on earth. May it be so.

In all your ways,
may you walk in step with the
Prince of Shalom,
and be empowered by his Spirit,
so that our Father's name
might be hallowed
and his will be done
as in heaven so on earth.
May it be so.

About Mark Greene

Ex-New York adman, ex-vice-principal of the London School of Theology, ex-director of LICC, Mark is now their Mission Champion, focused on expanding the practice of everyday mission in the UK.

A global pioneer for workplace ministry and whole-life discipleship, Mark has produced a wide range of books and resources including *Thank God It's Monday*, *Fruitfulness on the Frontline*, and *Probably the Best Idea in the World*. He's married to Katriina, a Finn. Mark relaxes to films, fiction, and dance music. He does a reasonable imitation of Mr Bean and a terrible one of Sean Connery. His wife wishes it was the other way round. His three adult children wish he wouldn't do either.

About LICC

How can we make a difference for Christ in our ordinary, everyday lives?

About 98% of UK Christians aren't in church-paid work - that's most of us. And we spend 95% of our time away from church – at work, school, home, down the pub, the shops, the gym - much of it with people who don't know Jesus.

The London Institute for Contemporary Christianity seeks to empower ordinary Christians, combining biblical insight with cultural understanding, to create frameworks, skills, and practices that help them flourish and show the difference Jesus makes - right where they are.

licc.org.uk

Follow @liccltd on Twitter, Facebook, Instagram and Linkedin.
View our videos and events @liccmedia on Youtube.
hello@licc.org.uk | 020 7399 9555